KELP

THE UNDERWATER FOREST!

By Patricia Fletcher

Gareth Stevens
PUBLISHING

Please visit our website, www.garethstevens.com. For a free color catalog of all our high-quality books, call toll free 1-800-542-2595 or fax 1-877-542-2596.

Cataloging-in-Publication Data

Names: Fletcher, Patricia.
Title: Kelp: the underwater forest! / Patricia Fletcher.
Description: New York : Gareth Stevens Publishing, 2017. | Series: world's weirdest plants | Includes index.
Identifiers: ISBN 9781482456141 (pbk.) | ISBN 9781482456288 (library bound) | ISBN 9781482456271 (6 pack)
Subjects: LCSH: Kelp bed ecology–Juvenile literature. | Kelps–Juvenile literature.
Classification: LCC QH541.5.K4 F54 2017 | DDC 577.7'8–dc23

First Edition

Published in 2017 by
Gareth Stevens Publishing
111 East 14th Street, Suite 349
New York, NY 10003

Copyright © 2017 Gareth Stevens Publishing

Designer: Katelyn E. Reynolds
Editor: Kristen Nelson and Joan Stoltman

Photo credits: Cover, p. 1 Ralph A. Clevenger/Corbis/Getty Images; cover, pp. 1–24 (background) Conny Sjostrom/Shutterstock.com; cover, pp. 1–24 (sign elements) A Sk/Shutterstock.com; pp. 5, 11 (main), 13 Douglas Klug/Moment Open/Getty Images; p. 7 ekler/Shutterstock.com; p. 9 Reinhard Dirscherl/ullstein bild via Getty Images; p. 11 (inset) Jim Agronick/Shutterstock.com; p. 15 Norbert Wu/Minden Pictures/Getty Images; p. 17 Joe Dovala/WaterFrame/Getty Images; p. 19 KGrif/Shutterstock.com; p. 21 (photo) Jeffrey L. Rotman/Corbis Documentary/Getty Images.

Printed in China

CPSIA compliance information: Batch #CW17GS : For further information contact Gareth Stevens, New York, New York at 1-800-542-2595.

CONTENTS

Words in the glossary appear in **bold** type
the first time they are used in the text.

A SWIM IN THE FOREST

When walking through a forest, you might look up to see the sun peeking through the tallest branches. Now, imagine *swimming* through a forest, looking up and seeing something similar. That's what it would be like inside a kelp forest!

Kelp aren't plants—but they're a lot like plants. Kelp are brown algae that grow plentifully under the right conditions. They have some odd parts and look pretty strange out of the water. But under the water, kelp forests are an important **habitat**!

SEEDS OF KNOWLEDGE

Algae are plantlike living things that are mostly found in water. They're protists, one of the main groups of living things on Earth.

4

Kelp is a kind of seaweed! "Seaweed" means any red, green, or brown algae that grow on shorelines.

5

LOOKING FOR KELP

Kelp forests are found in **shallow**, cool parts of Earth's oceans. Kelp forests exist off the coasts of South Africa, Australia, New Zealand, and the western coasts of North and South America. The kelp forests off California's shore are the most well-known near the United States.

Kelp often grows on **reefs** in water that's up to about 100 feet (30 m) deep. It may also grow onto the shore up to the point where the low tide comes in.

SEEDS OF KNOWLEDGE

The largest kelp forests are found in waters below 68°F (20°C).

WHERE ARE KELP FORESTS?

NORTH AMERICA

EUROPE

ASIA

Atlantic Ocean

Pacific Ocean

AFRICA

SOUTH AMERICA

Indian Ocean

■ kelp

AUSTRALIA

Southern Ocean

ANTARCTICA

Kelp forests are found where there are high levels of **nutrients** in the water.

7

KELP PARTS

Unlike plants, kelp doesn't have roots. At its base, it has a holdfast, which sticks to a rock or reef and keeps the kelp in place. Kelp also has a stipe, a part of kelp like a plant's stem that holds it up. Joined to the stipe are the blades, which are long and look like leaves.

Though its parts are slightly different, kelp makes food the same way plants do! Kelp uses sunlight to make its own food through **photosynthesis**.

SEEDS OF KNOWLEDGE

Kelp gathers sunlight for photosynthesis through its blades. Kelp **absorbs** other needed nutrients right from the water through the blades, too.

8

Bladders filled with gas at the base of kelp's blades help them float closer to the water's surface to absorb the most sunlight. They also keep the kelp upright in the water.

9

INSIDE THE FOREST

Kelp forests are full of life. The upper level of a kelp forest is the canopy, which is where the highest blades of kelp meet and cover the forest. Living in the canopy are crabs, snails, young fish, and many other small **organisms**.

In the middle level of the forest are bigger, predatory fish. What kinds of fish depend on where the kelp forest is found. The next level has other kinds of algae and shorter kelp.

SEEDS OF KNOWLEDGE

The kelp forest floor is home to ocean animals such as sponges and sea anemones.

The tallest kelp grows to the water's surface and then starts growing **horizontally** on top of the water!

garibaldi fish in a kelp forest off Catalina Island

A SAFE PLACE...TO EAT!

Kelp forests give many animals **protection** from predators that might want to eat them. The forests also act as a nursery, or place where young ocean animals can grow. Kelp forests give fish, seals, otters, and even seabirds cover from rough waters and storms.

Kelp forests are helpful to people, too. They protect shorelines from waves. Also, many kinds of fish that people like to eat live in kelp forests. Abalone, snapper, wrasse, rockfish, and rock lobsters all live in the kelp forest habitat.

Birds, seals, and whales love to eat where there's a kelp forest! There are lots of small bugs, fish, and other small organisms to dine on.

13

LINKS IN A CHAIN

Not many animals eat kelp forests, but sea urchins gobble right through the holdfast of kelp for dinner! Sea urchins are eaten by sea otters, making kelp a part of an important ocean **food chain**.

However, sometimes sea otters are killed for their fur. By the 1950s, the southern sea otter had nearly died out near California! Without them, the sea urchin population grew too fast and ate more kelp than usual. The kelp forests took years to get back to what they were.

SEEDS OF KNOWLEDGE

Kelp **reproduction** includes tiny bodies called spores. Some plants, such as ferns, also use these instead of seeds. Weird!

Kelp can be torn loose from kelp forests. When it washes up onshore or sinks to the bottom of the ocean, it becomes food for animals there, too.

GIANT KELP

In the best conditions, one kind of kelp can grow to be 175 feet (53 m) tall! Giant kelp is one of the fastest-growing living things on Earth. It can grow about 2 feet (0.6 m) in 1 day! It grows best in turbulent, or choppy, water that's always bringing it fresh nutrients.

Giant kelp can be found in kelp forests off the coasts of California and Mexico, South America, New Zealand, and Australia.

SEEDS OF KNOWLEDGE

Kelp forests are mostly made up of giant kelp and bull kelp, though there are many kinds of kelp.

Scientists dive deep into the ocean to study the kelp forest habitat, including giant kelp.

KELP IN TROUBLE?

Overpopulation of sea urchins isn't the only problem faced by these weird and amazing underwater forests. Anything that affects how clear the water is, such as pollution, stops kelp from getting needed sunlight for photosynthesis. Pollution also affects the nutrient levels in kelp forests, which can harm their growth.

Global climate change, or the slow change in Earth's weather patterns over time, will likely have an affect on kelp as well. Kelp likes to grow in cooler water, but the world's oceans are warming up!

SEEDS OF KNOWLEDGE

Overfishing can harm the kelp forest habitat. Too many or too few of any animal or plant in a habitat can upset its balance!

Scientists aren't sure how warmer ocean waters will change kelp forests yet. Some say kelp might start growing in deeper or cooler water.

HELPFUL KELP

People use kelp for all sorts of things! A part of kelp cells called algin is used to thicken some foods. Kelp is used to make shampoo, toothpaste, and more. Much of the kelp people use, though, isn't taken from wild kelp forests because many of them are protected areas. Scientists study these protected kelp forests to learn how to keep these habitats healthy.

Kelp forests may look odd at first glance, but when you dive in, they're some of the most amazing forests on Earth!

SEEDS OF KNOWLEDGE

Off the coast of California, man-made reefs were put in the water in 2008 to try to help the kelp forests grow better there. It worked! Now there are acres of kelp forest.

THE PARTS OF KELP

- blade
- bladder
- stipe
- holdfast

harvesting kelp

GLOSSARY

absorb: to take in

bladder: a gas-filled part of certain algae that serves to help hold up the algae by floating

food chain: the way in which animals and plants pass energy within a community

habitat: the natural place where an organism lives

horizontally: in a manner level with the ground

nutrient: something a living thing needs to grow and stay alive

organism: a living thing

photosynthesis: the process of plants and algae that uses sunlight, the gas carbon dioxide, and water to make food

protection: the act of keeping safe

reef: a chain of rocks or coral, or a ridge of sand, at or near the water's surface

reproduction: when an animal creates another creature just like itself

shallow: not deep

FOR MORE INFORMATION

 Books

Johnson, Robin. *Oceans Inside Out.* New York, NY: Crabtree Publishing, 2015.

Lawrence, Ellen. *Water Plants: All Wet!* New York, NY: Bearport Publishing Company, Inc., 2016.

Websites

DragonflyTV: Kelp Forest
pbskids.org/dragonflytv/show/kelpforest.html
Check out this video about kelp forests, and learn even more about them.

Photo Gallery: Kelp Garden
ocean.nationalgeographic.com/ocean/photos/kelp-gardens/
See many photographs of amazing kelp forests.

INDEX